What are NFTs? - 4 YOU - The NFT comprehensive guidebook

NFT for investors, photographers, video producers, Graphic designers, illustrators, 3D artists, animators, - Game developers, programmers, filmmakers, producers, Musicians, composers, artisans, designers, architects, interior designers, scientists and researchers

Financial Specialist Holger Kiefer

Verlagslabel: Kiefer-Coaching
ISBN
Softcover 978-3-347-93455-9
Hardcover 978-3-347-93456-6
E-Book 978-3-347-93457-3

Printing and distribution on behalf of :
tredition GmbH, An der Strusbek 10, 22926 Ahrensburg, Germany.

A warm welcome to you,

You are about to receive a comprehensive reference book about NFT's, which will be indispensable for your entry into the almost infinite possibilities, which NFT's offer.

At the same time, however, you will also receive information about what you must pay attention to and what risks may be associated with it.

Use this guide, which explains the absolutely necessary technical terms in understandable language.

On purpose some topics were treated several times, in order to point out different points of view and to consolidate the knowledge about it, because in the long run it is also a workbook.

Not only for investors, but also for sportsmen, musicians and artists of all genres, NFT's offer the possibility of a fast monetizing without intermediate trade.

I wish you much success for your investments

Holger Kiefer

Inhaltsverzeichnis

I. Introduction to NFTs.....1
Definition of NFTs.....1
History and development of NFTs.....3
Expert opinions:.....5
Comparison with other digital assets.....6
II. How NFTs work.....8
Blockchain technology and NFTs.....8
Blockchain technology and NFTs in detail:.....10
Advantages and opportunities of NFT investments.....25
Smart Contracts and NFTs.....27
Tokenization of digital content.....29
III. applications of NFTs.....31
Art and culture.....31
Music industry.....34
Video Game Industry.....37
Sports.....39
Social Media.....43
IV. Investments in NFTs.....45
Advantages and opportunities of NFT investments.....45
Risks and challenges of NFT investments.....48
How to buy and sell NFTs.....51
How can a painter create his works with NFTs.....54
a) protect with NFTs.....54
b) sell as NFTs.....55
c) what are the costs of NTFs sales?.....56
How can a musician protect his works with NFTs?.....57
Protect and market through NTFs.....59
NFT marketplaces and platforms.....62

V. The future of NFTs....64
Forecasts and trends....64
1. growth of the NFT market....64
2. NFTs as a tool for content monetization....65
3. use of NFTs in the game industry....65
4. NFTs as proof of identity....65
5. further fields of application....66
Regulatory Risks....70
Risks related to authenticity and verification....71
Volatility and price risks....72
Market risks....73
Technical Risks....74
Fraud and Security Risks....74
Environmental Issues....74
How to buy and sell NFTs....77
Potential Applications and Developments....90
VII. Conclusion: Are NFTs the future?....92
VIII. Conclusion....94
Summary of key insights....94
Personal Assessment and Recommendations....98
VIIII. Anhang....100
Glossar....100
Known NFT offerings....104
Everydays: The First 5000 Days....104
Bibliography:....108
Artikel:....110
Websites:....111
Links and Resources....112

I. Introduction to NFTs

Definition of NFTs.

A Non-Fungible Token (NFT) is a digital asset based on blockchain technology that is unique.

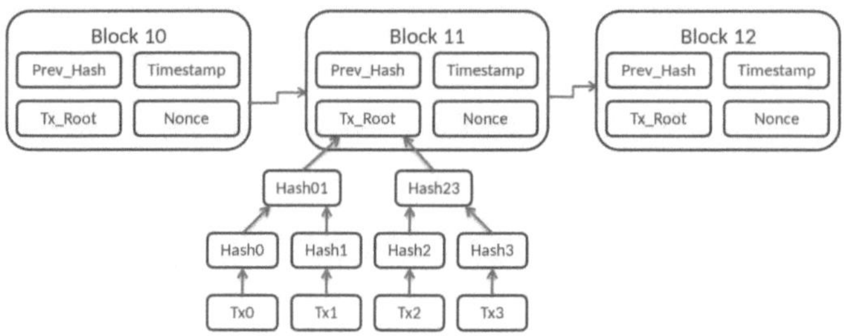

Blockchain is a type of decentralized and distributed digital ledger system that stores information in blocks and connects them through a network of computers. Each block contains a group of transactions or information that are cryptographically linked to prevent tampering or modification. Once a block is created, it is stored in the blockchain and cannot be altered, ensuring the integrity and security of the information stored in it. This makes blockchain particularly useful for things like financial transactions, identity management, and data storage, where security and confidentiality are critical.

Unlike cryptocurrencies like Bitcoin, which are interchangeable, each NFT has a unique identity and value. NFTs are often used to represent and sell digital artwork, music files, videos, or other digital content such as even virtual properties in online games. Each NFT contains information that proves its uniqueness and ownership. Basically, NFTs work like digital certificates or ownership deeds for digital content.
You'll get more information as we go along.

History and development of NFTs

The first NFTs were introduced on the Ethereum blockchain in 2017. The CryptoKitties project, which allowed users to collect and breed digital cats, was one of the first and most successful NFT projects.

Since then, NFTs have become a major trend in the crypto and art scene. In 2021, the NFT market reached a record high with a total volume of over $2 billion. Many artists and musicians are using NFTs as a new way to monetize digital artwork and music and protect their work. More recently, major corporations such as the NBA and NFL have also begun using NFTs to sell collectibles and merchandise. The history and evolution of NFTs is still young, and new applications and technologies are expected to develop in the coming years that will further transform the NFT market.

Expert opinions:

"The idea that you, as the creator, have proof that you are the owner of a particular piece of digital art or music is pretty revolutionary."
- Kevin Chou, CEO of Rally.io

"NFTs offer the opportunity for artists to finally get paid appropriately for their work." - Anne Spalter, digital artist and professor at the Rhode Island School of Design

"The potential of NFTs is huge, especially in industries like arts and culture, where it has often been difficult in the past to clarify ownership of digital works."

- Lorne Lantz, co-founder of Blockchain Studios

Comparison with other digital assets

Compared to other digital assets such as cryptocurrencies, NFTs have some unique characteristics. Cryptocurrencies such as Bitcoin are fungible, meaning they are interchangeable and have the same value. In contrast, NFTs are unique and not interchangeable because each NFT has a unique identity and properties that distinguish it from other NFTs. Another important difference is that NFTs represent specific digital content, while cryptocurrencies have no real or physical value.

Compared to traditional physical collectibles such as paintings or baseball cards, NFTs provide a better way to prove the authenticity and ownership of digital content. NFTs also allow artists and musicians to profit directly from their work without relying on intermediaries such as galleries or record labels.

However, there are also some challenges and risks associated with NFTs. The market for NFTs is still young and unregulated, which can lead to high price volatility and fraud. In addition, it is difficult to determine the long-term value of NFTs, as it depends on many factors such as the popularity of the digital content and the demand for NFTs.

II. How NFTs work

Blockchain technology and NFTs

Blockchain technology is the engine behind NFTs. NFTs are stored and transmitted on a blockchain, which allows them to be unique and tamper-proof. A blockchain is basically a distributed digital database that consists of blocks that are chained together. Each block contains a specific amount of data and is linked to the previous block through a cryptographic hash function. This creates an immutable record that cannot be tampered with or corrupted.

The Ethereum blockchain is typically used for NFTs because it allows developers to create smart contracts that specify the properties and rules for each NFT.

Smart contracts are programs that are executed automatically when certain conditions are met. For example, they can ensure that the seller of an NFT receives a certain percentage of the sale price or that the owner of an NFT has certain usage rights.

The use of blockchain technology and smart contracts makes trading NFTs more secure and transparent. Each transaction is recorded in the blockchain and can be viewed by any user. This ensures that each NFT is unique and authentic and that the ownership of the NFT is clearly documented.

Blockchain technology and NFTs in detail:

- - What is blockchain technology? Blockchain technology is a distributed database technology that allows digital transactions to be recorded securely and transparently without the need for a central authority. The blockchain consists of a chain of blocks that are linked together and record transactions.

  - How does blockchain technology work? Blockchain technology works by recording transactions in blocks and securely linking these blocks together using cryptographic techniques. Each block contains a hash of the previous block, creating an immutable chain of blocks.

  - How is blockchain technology related to NFTs? NFTs are digital assets created and traded using blockchain technology. Blockchain technology enables secure and transparent tracking of NFT transactions and unique identification of NFTs.

  - What types of blockchains are used for NFTs? Public blockchains such as Ethereum and Binance Smart Chain are generally used for NFTs. These blockchains are decentralized and allow NFTs to be created and tracked in a secure and transparent manner.

- How can the use of blockchain technology improve NFTs? Using blockchain technology for NFTs enables unique identification of NFTs, tracking of transactions, and securing ownership. This makes trading NFTs easier and more secure.

- What challenges need to be considered when using blockchain technology for NFTs? One challenge with using blockchain technology for NFTs is that blockchains are typically energy intensive and can incur high fees for transactions. In addition, it can be difficult to interoperate NFTs on different blockchains.

Another aspect driving demand for NFTs is their role as an investment vehicle. Many investors have realized that NFTs can offer significant potential for value appreciation and have begun to invest in NFTs. Some NFTs have already fetched huge sums at auction, and it's no secret that NFTs can be an attractive way to make money.

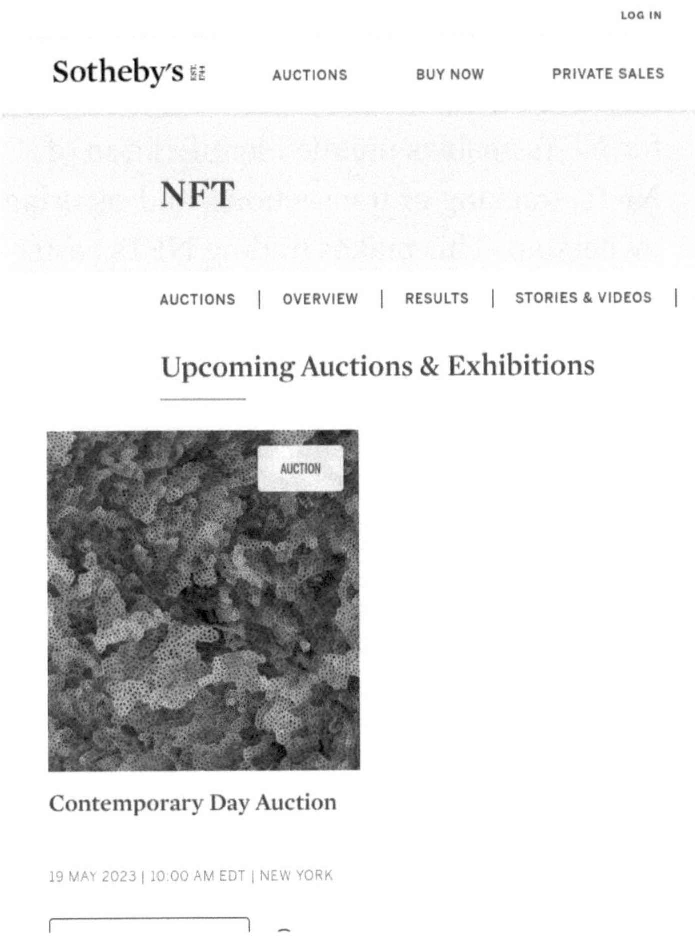

However, NFTs also have risks and challenges for investors. Because the market is still relatively young and unregulated, there are fraudulent practices and uncertainties associated with the pricing of NFTs. It is important for investors to carefully research and rely on the valuation of NFTs before investing.

There are also concerns about the sustainability of NFTs and the impact on the environment, as blockchain technology consumes a significant amount of energy. However, some platforms have begun to switch to environmentally friendly methods to address these concerns.

NFTs also have implications for the arts and culture sector, as they offer new ways to monetize digital works. Artists and creators can now sell their digital works as NFTs and receive direct support from their fans, rather than depending on third-party vendors. This has led to a democratization of the art market and allows artists to monetize their creations in ways that were not possible before.

Overall, NFTs have the potential to change the way

we own, trade, and monetize digital assets. They offer new opportunities for investors, artists, and creators, and have already impacted the arts and culture sector. While there are still challenges and uncertainties, the popularity of NFTs is expected to continue to grow in the coming years, spawning new applications and developments.

In terms of the music industry, NFTs have the potential to change the way musicians and artists interact with their fans and manage their intellectual property. An example of this is Grammy winner and rapper "RAC" who launched an NFT sale of 3 unique songs he created specifically for sale in May 2021. The NFTs were created with unique artwork and access to exclusive experiences like a personal remix that was only available to the buyer. The sale took only a few minutes and generated total sales of 33 ETH (about $63,000 USD).

Another example is Kings of Leon, a well-known American band that released its new album as an NFT in March 2021. The sale included three different NFT packages with different types of exclusive content such as limited vinyl sets, a digital artwork, and exclusivc audio clips. The band said they decided to sell it as NFT to "present the music in a new way and reward fans who are interested in it."

1.21 T $ Bitcoin-Kurs 28,710.16 $ 0.94% Ethereum-Kurs 1,871.62 $ 1.31% Cardano-Kurs 0.391431 $ 1.04% XRP-Kurs 0.460334 $

BTC-ECHO

Ethereum-Skalierung

Zero-Knowledge-Rollups im Vergleich. Jetzt im Magazin lesen!

Themen Magazin Podcasts Reviews Academy Events Investieren Kurse Bitcoin kaufen

Themen Magazin Podcasts Reviews Academy Events Investieren Kurse

Rock'NFT'Roll

Rockband "Kings of Leon" bringt Album als NFT heraus

Die Rockband "Kings of Leon" veröffentlicht ihr nächstes Album auch als NFT. Damit leistet die Band Pionierarbeit.

von Daniel Hoppmann
04.03.2021, 14:10

TEILEN

Bitcoin-Kurs 28,710.16 $

However, there are also concerns about the impact of NFTs on the music industry, particularly with regard to the possibility of piracy and unauthorized use of music. As a result, some artists are skeptical of NFTs and fear that they may do more harm than good.

Overall, however, the use of NFTs in the music industry shows the potential for a new kind of interaction between artists and fans, as well as innovative and unique ways to sell and use intellectual property.
Another way NFTs are being used in the music industry is through the creation of NFT platforms that allow musicians to sell their music directly to their fans. Some platforms also offer the ability to sell rare music collections, concert recordings, and other exclusive content.

An example of this is the NFT platform "YellowHeart," which was founded by music manager Josh Katz.

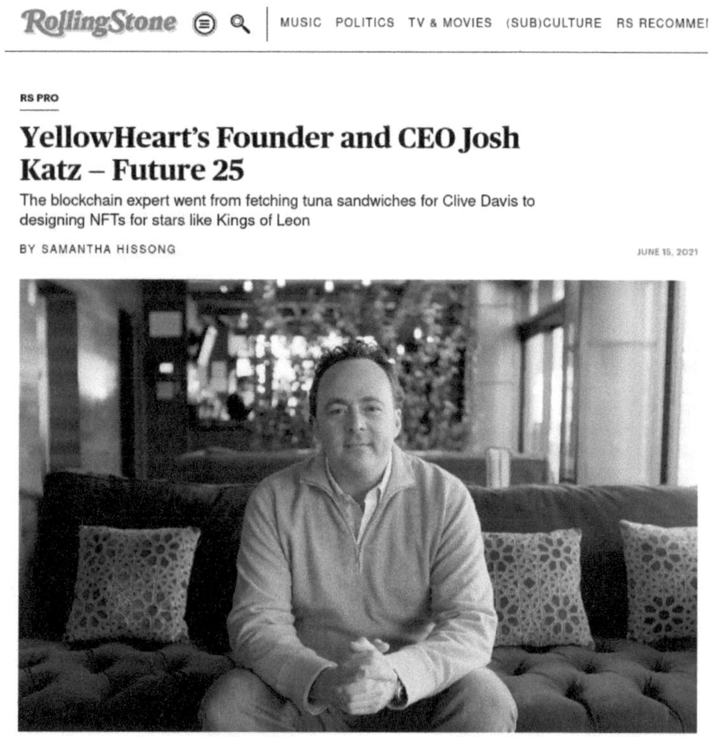

RollingStone MUSIC POLITICS TV & MOVIES (SUB)CULTURE RS RECOMME

RS PRO

YellowHeart's Founder and CEO Josh Katz – Future 25

The blockchain expert went from fetching tuna sandwiches for Clive Davis to designing NFTs for stars like Kings of Leon

BY SAMANTHA HISSONG

JUNE 15, 2021

https://www.rollingstone.com

The platform offers artists the opportunity to create NFTs and sell them to fans. The NFTs can include various types of exclusive content, such as digital access to concerts, special merchandise, or even musicians' personal items like guitars and drums.

For a guide to music's potential crypto boom, visit

https://www.rollingstone.com

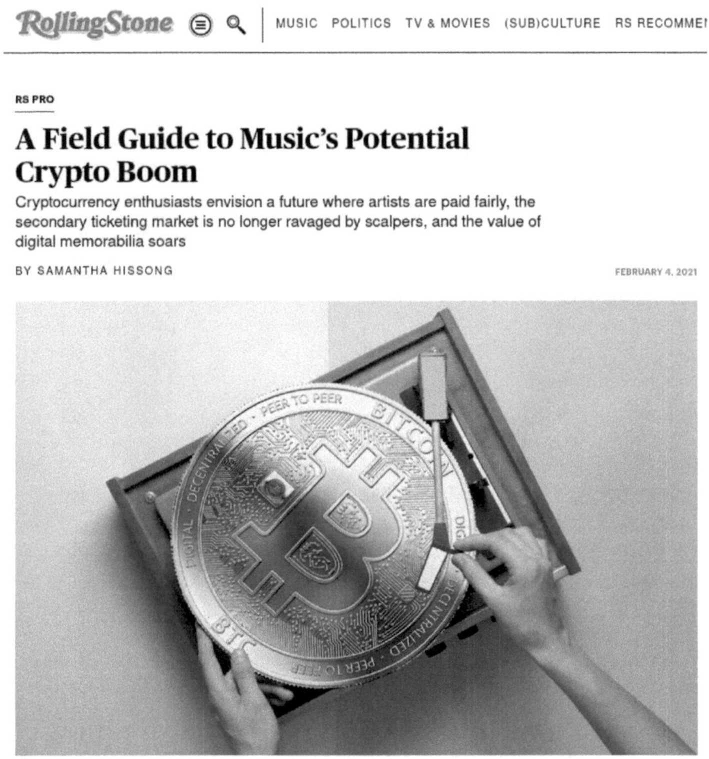

RollingStone | MUSIC POLITICS TV & MOVIES (SUB)CULTURE RS RECOMME

RS PRO

A Field Guide to Music's Potential Crypto Boom

Cryptocurrency enthusiasts envision a future where artists are paid fairly, the secondary ticketing market is no longer ravaged by scalpers, and the value of digital memorabilia soars

BY SAMANTHA HISSONG FEBRUARY 4, 2021

Cryptocurrency enthusiasts envision a future where artists are paid fairly, the secondary card market is no longer plagued by scalpers, and the value of digital memorabilia skyrockets

What if hundreds of thousands of music industry artists - who are especially strapped for cash when they can't tour, as they are right now in the Covid 19 pandemic - didn't have to wait a cripplingly long time to receive their royalties , but could receive streaming money immediately? Extend this thought experiment: what if there was a "merch royalty" so that the artist gets a cut every time a branded hoodie or piece of art is resold, or a system that ensures accurate paychecks for musicians?

Crypto advocates want to develop a new financial system for music that can support real-time revenue streams and ultimately give much more power to the individual artist. The average music fan can easily be put off by these talks: Cryptocurrency is, well, cryptic, and articles on the subject are usually filled with jargon and long digressions. So Rolling Stonehas explored the landscape, and with the help of experts like Zach Katz, Shara Senderoff, Adam Alpert, and RAC, we'll walk you through the origins, potential applications, and latest developments of what crypto can mean for music.

The video game industry has also begun to use NFTs to enhance the game world and game mechanics. NFTs can be used in games as unique items or weapons that can only be owned by one player.

These items can also be traded on the market, creating a secondary market for digital assets.

An example of a game that uses NFTs is "Axie Infinity," a blockchain-based game where players can collect creatures, breed them, and compete against other players. Each creature is stored as an NFT on the Ethereum blockchain and can be bought and sold on the market. Due to the growing popularity of the game, the prices of rare creatures on the market have increased, making it a lucrative investment for players.

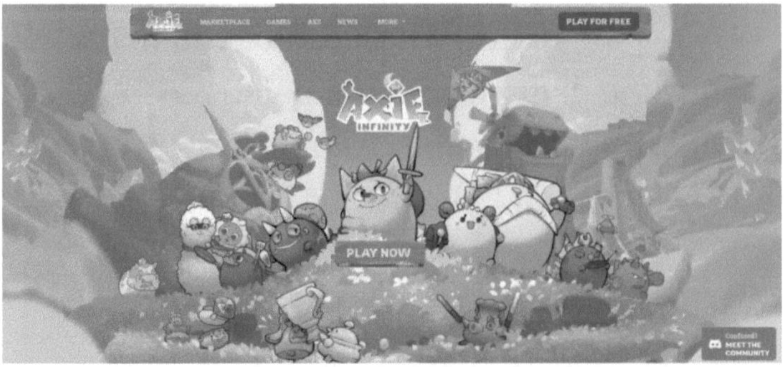

There are also many opportunities for NFTs in sports. Some sports teams have already started to use NFTs to engage their fans more closely and create unique fan experiences.

For example, the National Basketball Association (NBA) has developed an NFT platform called "NBA Top Shot" where fans can purchase and collect digital trading cards of NBA players. These cards contain highlights from games and can be traded on the secondary market.

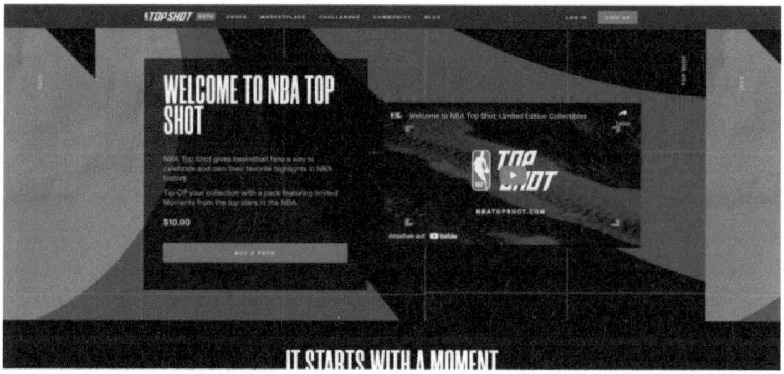

In addition to these application areas, there is also potential for NFTs in other areas such as.

- Social media,
- fashion and even in
- Science.

Overall, there are many opportunities for NFTs to change the way we own, trade and experience digital assets.

Advantages and opportunities of NFT investments

Compared to other digital assets, such as cryptocurrencies, NFTs are often seen as a promising new approach to monetizing content and creating value. Cryptocurrencies such as Bitcoin and Ethereum are considered fungible tokens because each token is the same within the network and has the same value. In contrast, NFTs are unique and non-exchangeable because they are linked to a specific digital asset such as an image, a video, or a piece of music.

This uniqueness and exclusivity makes NFTs particularly attractive to artists, musicians, and other creators looking to monetize their digital works. NFTs allow owners to present their works as distinctive collectibles, creating unique experiences and value.

The blockchain technology on which NFTs are based also offers several advantages over other digital assets. For example, NFTs are typically more secure and transparent because the blockchain records the ownership and transaction history of each token. This ensures that NFTs are authentic and cannot be counterfeited or duplicated.

However, there are also some challenges and risks associated with NFTs. For example, there are concerns about the energy consumption and environmental impact of proof-of-work blockchain networks such as Ethereum, which are commonly used to create NFTs. In addition, there are concerns about the scalability and interoperability of NFTs that could make them difficult to use and trade more broadly.

Overall, however, it is clear that NFTs are an exciting new approach to digital content creation and monetization that has the potential to change the way we view and trade digital art, music, and other creative works.

Smart Contracts and NFTs

Smart contracts are an important part of NFTs because they define the rules and properties of each NFT and are executed automatically when certain conditions are met. A smart contract is basically a self-executing code stored on the blockchain that automatically executes certain actions when the conditions it specifies are met.

For example, for NFTs, smart contracts can specify who owns the NFT and what rights the owner has to the NFT. They can also determine how the NFT can be traded and who gets what shares of the sale proceeds. In addition, smart contracts can also include a set of conditions and rules that can restrict or expand the use of the NFT.

Another advantage of smart contracts is that they make trading NFTs easier and safer. When an NFT is sold on a trading platform, the smart contract can automatically transfer the purchase price to the seller once the NFT is transferred to the buyer. This ensures that both parties have fulfilled the terms of the trade and that the seller receives the agreed amount.

Overall, smart contracts play an important role in the creation and management of NFTs, as they enable NFTs to be unique and secure, and ensure that all parties involved in transactions are protected.

Tokenization of digital content

Tokenization of digital content is an important aspect of NFTs. Essentially, tokenization means that a piece of digital content is divided into unique, identifiable tokens that are stored on the blockchain. Each token corresponds to a unique piece of digital content and has a unique identifier that distinguishes it from other tokens.

Tokenization of digital content allows owners to monetize their content in a new way. They can convert their content into NFTs and then offer them for sale on an NFT trading platform. When a buyer purchases an NFT, they gain ownership of a unique piece of digital content.

Tokenization of digital content can be used for a variety of content, including artwork, music, videos, games, or even virtual real estate. It can allow owners to market and monetize their content in a new way by selling it directly to their fans or customers.

Another benefit of tokenizing digital content is that it allows owners to better protect and control their content. Because each token is uniquely identifiable, owners can determine exactly who owns their content and what rights the owners have to the content. This can help reduce piracy and misuse of digital content and give owners more control over their works.

III. applications of NFTs

Art and culture

Artworks have long been collectibles and objects of speculation, but NFTs have changed the way artworks are created, sold, and traded. Through the use of NFTs, digital artworks can be viewed as unique and non-interchangeable entities, similar to traditional artworks.

A well-known example of the success of NFTs in the art world is digital artist Beeple, who held an auction at Christie's in March 2021 and sold his work "Everydays: The First 5000 Days" for $69 million. This was the first time Christie's auctioned a purely digital artwork as an NFT.
Another example is musician and artist Grimes, who sold a collection of NFT artwork in February 2021 that raised more than $6 million in just 20 minutes.

NFTs have grown in importance in recent years, particularly in the arts and culture sector. Artists and cultural institutions can use NFTs to sell digital artwork, music and other cultural content directly to collectors and fans.

A major advantage of NFTs for artworks is that they offer the ability to verify the authenticity and uniqueness of a digital artwork. Since each NFT is uniquely identifiable, a buyer can be sure that they own the original work and not simply a copy or a fake. This can increase the appeal and value of digital artworks and facilitate commerce in the field.

NFTs also allow artists to profit directly from their works without relying on traditional distribution channels such as galleries or record labels. They can sell their works directly to their fans and collectors and receive their income from these sales. This can help reduce income inequality in the arts and culture sector and democratize access to artworks for a wider audience.

In addition, NFTs can also help cultural institutions such as museums and libraries digitize and monetize their collections. They can create NFTs that represent unique parts of their collections and then offer them for sale on a commerce platform. This can help these institutions create new revenue streams and make their collections accessible to a wider audience.

Overall, NFTs in the arts and culture sector offer a variety of opportunities for artists, collectors, and institutions to monetize, protect, and market digital content.

Music industry

NFTs can also play an important role in the music industry. Artists and record labels can use NFTs to sell their music and other audiovisual content directly to fans.

Similar to the arts sector, NFTs allow musicians to profit directly from their works and rely on traditional distribution channels such as record labels or streaming services. They can sell their music directly to their fans and receive their revenue from those sales. NFTs can also help artists build a closer relationship with their fans by offering unique, personalized NFTs that provide special benefits or access to exclusive content.

In addition, NFTs can also help record labels and record companies create new revenue streams. They can create NFTs that represent unique parts of their music collections and then offer them for sale on a commerce platform. This can help record companies and labels diversify their revenues and better support their artists.

NFTs can also help protect the copyrights of musicians and artists. Each NFT is uniquely identifiable, making it harder to illegally copy or distribute music or other content. This can help ensure that musicians and artists are paid fairly for their work and that their work is not used without their permission.

Overall, NFTs in the music industry offer a new way for artists and record labels to monetize digital content and more closely engage their fans.
One example of the use of NFTs in the music industry is rapper and singer Post Malone, who released a collection of NFTs in April 2021 that included digital artwork, music, and an exclusive concert ticket.

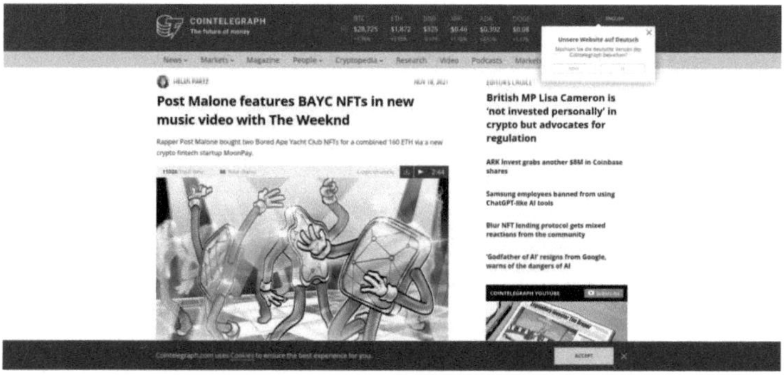

https://cointelegraph.com/

Video Game Industry

The video game industry is another example of an industry that can benefit from NFTs. In video games, NFTs can be used as digital collectibles or as access to exclusive content.

One example is rare in-game items, such as weapons or skins, that are hard to find and popular with collectors. These items can be tokenized as NFTs and sold directly to players. This makes it easier for players to acquire these rare items, and developers can profit directly from the sales.

In addition, NFTs can also be used to tokenize content such as game characters, levels, or other game content. This allows developers to sell their content directly to players and receive their revenue from the sales. NFTs can also be used to give players exclusive access to special features or events in the game.

NFTs can also help increase the security of in-game transactions, as each transaction is verified through blockchain technology. This can help players invest more securely in buying and selling digital items.

Overall, NFTs in the video game industry offer a new way for developers to monetize their digital content and more closely engage their players.

Sports

NFTs can also play a growing role in the sports sector. Especially in the area of sports memorabilia and collectibles, such as limited edition jerseys, shoes or other equipment, NFTs can be used.

By tokenizing these collectibles as NFTs, they can be uniquely and traceably identified on the blockchain. This gives collectors greater confidence and security when buying and selling collectibles. It can also help collectibles gain more value because they can be identified and verified as unique on the blockchain.

NFTs can also be used to manage rights and licenses in the sports sector. For example, teams or leagues could create NFTs to allow fans to purchase rights to a specific action, such as a highlight or goal. This can help fans feel more connected to their team or favorite sport and increase engagement and fan loyalty.

Another area of application for NFTs in sports is in fantasy sports games, where NFTs can be used as virtual players. This allows players to create their

COINTELEGRAPH
auf Deutsch

BTC	ETH	BNB	XRP
€26.157	€1.705	€295	€0,42
+3,59%	+3,37%	-0,99%	+0,81%

Nachrichten ⌄ Politik ⌄ Unternehmen ⌄ Märkte ⌄ Markt-Tools ⌄ Branch

ZHIYUAN SUN 11 JAN 2022

Dreifacher NBA-Champion Andre Iguodala lässt sich in Krypto bezahlen

Iguodala erklärte, er werde auch BTC im Wert von 1 Million US-Dollar an seine Fans verschenken, um die Akzeptanz der Kryptowährung zu fördern.

Am Montag kündigte Andre Iguodala, dreimaliger NBA-Champion und Basketballprofi bei den Golden State Warriors, über Twitter an, er werde einen Teil seines geschätzten Jahresgehalts von 2,647 Millionen US-Dollar in Bitcoin (BTC) erhalten. Iguodala fügte hinzu, er werde BTC im Wert von 1 Million US-Dollar an seine Fans verteilen, um die Akzeptanz der digitalen Währung zu fördern. Die Zahlungen sollen über die Cash-App von Block (ehemals Square) abgewickelt werden.

own virtual teams of NFT players and compete against other players in a virtual league.

Overall, in the sports space, NFTs can help increase

the value of collectibles and other sports items, as well as give fans and players a better way to monetize and manage digital content.

One example of this is NBA player Andre Iguodala, who released a collection of NFTs in May 2021 that gave his fans access to exclusive content such as a visit to his locker room or dinner with him.

Social Media

Social media platforms have already started to integrate NFTs. Here, NFTs can be used as digital items, such as emojis or stickers. These digital collectibles can be purchased by users and used in their social media.

Another application area is the use of NFTs for identity management. NFTs can be used as unique digital identity credentials stored on the blockchain.

This allows users to prove their digital identity while protecting their data.

In addition, NFTs can also help monetize content on social media platforms. Artists, influencers, or other content creators can sell their digital content as NFTs to be supported directly by their fans.

This can help content creators become less dependent on advertising revenue or other monetization opportunities.

NFTs can also be used to create digital collectibles and limited edition content on social media platforms. For example, limited edition photos or videos can be created as NFTs and sold to fans.

Overall, NFTs on social media platforms offer a new way for users to manage their digital identity, monetize content, and collect digital collectibles.

IV. Investments in NFTs

Advantages and opportunities of NFT investments

NFTs have experienced a lot of hype in recent years and have become a sought-after investment. Here are some advantages and opportunities of NFT investments:

1. uniqueness: NFTs are unique digital assets stored on the blockchain. This means they cannot be easily copied, which increases the value of the NFT. Especially in the case of artworks or other limited editions, this can lead to a high increase in value.

2. Potentially high returns: Some NFTs have historically commanded high prices, resulting in high returns for investors. For some works of art or collectibles, investors can increase the value of their investment many times over within months or years.

Because NFTs are unique and non-fungible digital assets, they can increase in value over time due to their rarity and demand. An example of this is the NFT artwork "Everydays: The First 5000 Days" by artist Beeple, which sold for $69 million at Christie's in March 2021.

3. diversification: NFT investments can be a way to diversify the portfolio and invest in new assets. In particular, for investors already investing in cryptocurrencies or other digital assets, NFTs can be a complement.

4. access to new markets:
NFTs allow investors to invest in new markets that were previously difficult to access. For example, investors can invest in artwork from emerging artists or limited edition video games.

5. strong community: many NFT projects have a strong community of supporters who support the development and success of the project. This can help increase the value of the NFT and provide a higher return on investment.

However, it is important to note that NFT

investments also come with risks. The NFT market is highly volatile, and the value of an NFT can fluctuate greatly. Investors should therefore always conduct thorough research and risk analysis before investing in NFTs.

Risks and challenges of NFT investments

NFT investments can also present risks and challenges. Here are some important aspects that investors should consider:

1. volatility: the NFT market is highly volatile, which means that the value of an NFT can fluctuate greatly. An NFT that has a high value today may suddenly lose value tomorrow.

2. lack of liquidity: unlike traditional assets such as stocks or bonds, NFTs can be harder to sell. It can be difficult to find buyers for a particular NFT, especially when the market is saturated.

3. High costs: some NFTs have high transaction costs, which can make buying and selling NFTs expensive. These costs can have a negative impact on returns.

4. Lack of regulation: the NFT market is currently largely unregulated, which means that there are no

clear standards on how NFTs should be valued. This can lead to investors having difficulty determining the value of an NFT.

5. Technological risks: Since NFTs are based on blockchain technology, they are susceptible to technological risks such as hacks, bugs, and malware.

6. Fraud: As with any new market, there are scams in the NFT market. Therefore, investors should always be cautious and conduct thorough research before investing in NFTs.

7. Environmental Issues: The process of creating NFTs is very energy intensive and can cause a significant environmental impact. This may cause investors to have concerns about the sustainability of NFTs.

8. lack of liquidity: the NFT market is not yet as liquid as other markets, which means it may be more difficult to buy or sell NFTs.

Overall, investors should consider all factors when deciding to invest in NFTs and carefully weigh whether the potential benefits outweigh the risks.

How to buy and sell NFTs

If you decide to buy or sell NFTs, there are some important steps you should follow:

1. to invest in NFTs, you need to buy an NFT. This can be done on various platforms and marketplaces that allow you to trade NFTs. Buying an NFT is usually done through a cryptocurrency such as Ether or Bitcoin.

2. Create a Wallet: Before you can buy or sell NFTs, you need a wallet address to store your digital assets. There are several types of wallets, including online wallets, desktop wallets, and hardware wallets. Choose a wallet that suits your needs and is secure.

3. Register on an NFT marketplace: there are several NFT marketplaces where you can buy and sell NFTs. Some of the most popular are OpenSea, Rarible, SuperRare, and Nifty Gateway. Register on a marketplace and verify your account.

4. Find NFTs that you want to buy: Search the marketplace for NFTs you want to buy. You can search by artists, themes, or categories.

5. Bid on the NFT: When you find an NFT you want to bid on, place a bid. If you place the highest bid, you will get the NFT.

6. lack of liquidity: the NFT market is not yet as liquid as other markets, which means it may be more difficult to buy or sell NFTs.

7. To sell an NFT, you need to list it on an NFT platform or NFT marketplace. You can set the price of the NFT and wait until a buyer is willing to pay the price.

8. Sell your NFTs: If you want to sell NFTs, make sure you provide the details of the NFT as well as the selling price. You can also set an auction price to get the highest bid.

9. Check the transaction details: check all the transaction details before making a payment or

selling an NFT. Make sure you are paying or receiving the correct amount and that the transaction is secure and confirmed.

It is important to learn about the processes and policies of the NFT marketplace where you plan to trade. Each marketplace has its own rules and fees, and you should be aware of them before making a transaction.

How can a painter create his works with NFTs

a) protect with NFTs

An artist can protect his works with NFTs by digitally verifying the rights to his work and registering them on the blockchain in the form of an NFT. This makes the work unalterable, indelible, and publicly accessible. Anyone holding the NFT has the right to own and trade the original work, while the artist retains control over who can use or reproduce the work.

To do this, the artist can use an NFT verification service such as OpenSea or SuperRare to digitize their work and sell it as an NFT. In doing so, the NFT verification service will create a digital copy of the work that will be registered with a unique token on the blockchain. The NFT verification service will then sell the NFT and pay the artist with a percentage of the sale price.

It is important to note that the NFT only protects the

right to the digital artwork, not the physical work itself. It is therefore advisable to protect the physical work separately, for example by storing it in a secure safe and covering it with insurance.

b) sell as NFTs

An artist can sell their work as NFTs by offering it on an NFT marketplace such as OpenSea, Rarible, or SuperRare. The artist must first digitize the work and register it as an NFT in order to offer it on the marketplace. The selling price of the NFT depends on the value and demand of the work.

When an NFT is sold, the artist receives a percentage of the sale price. Since most NFT marketplaces are based on the Ethereum blockchain, transactions are conducted in Ether. The artist can then convert their Ether into fiat currency or exchange it for cryptocurrencies, depending on their personal preference.

It is important to note that the NFT sale does not affect the physical work. The buyer only receives the digital NFT and the associated right to own and trade the work. The physical work must be sold separately if desired.

c) what are the costs of NTFs sales?

The cost of creating and selling an NFT may vary depending on the platform and the specific features. Some platforms charge a fee for creating and selling NFTs, while others may charge a percentage fee for selling the NFT.

The cost may also depend on whether the platform requires the use of a specific cryptocurrency to conduct transactions. Note that it's difficult to give an exact amount, as costs can vary widely. It is best to research and compare the fees charged by each platform before choosing one.

How can a musician protect his works with NFTs?

A musician can protect his works using NFTs by registering them on the blockchain platform. For this purpose, he can use a specific platform specialized in selling music NFTs, or he can use a general platform designed for trading different types of NFTs.

To ensure that the NFTs represent his original works, the musician can usually embed information about the work, including the title, length, date of creation, and genre, in the metadata of the NFT. This ensures that the NFT represents only the original work and not a duplicate or copy.

In addition, the musician can also add special features to the NFT, such as access rights to exclusive content or private concerts that are only available to owners of the NFT.

The cost of creating an NFT depends on the platform chosen and the features included. Some platforms may charge a fee for uploading and registering

NFTs, while others may charge a commission for selling NFTs. It is therefore important to compare the different platforms and their fees to find the best option for your needs.

Protect and market through NTFs

For which professional groups it is suitable to protect or market their works or productions through NTs?
It is appropriate for a variety of professions to protect or market their work or productions through NFTs. These include:

1. artists and designers: NFTs can help increase the value of artwork and design objects by proving ownership and authenticity.

2. musicians and DJs: NFTs can be used to mark and sell music tracks, remixes, and other audio files as rare collectibles.

3. authors and writers: NFTs can be used to help protect copyright in works and facilitate the sale of limited edition books or e-books.

4. video game developers: NFTs can help enable and facilitate the trade of in-game items and other digital assets within video games.

5. photographers and filmmakers: NFTs can help increase the value of photographs and film productions by proving authenticity and ownership of these works.

6. influencers and social media stars: NFTs can help increase the value of unique digital content, such as memes or viral videos, by proving authenticity and ownership.

7. collectors: NFTs can help collectors collect rare and unique items by proving ownership and authenticity of collectibles.

There are a variety of professions that could benefit from using NFTs to protect and market their work. Here are some examples:

- Writers and authors
- Photographers and video producers
- Graphic designers and illustrators
- 3D artists and animators
- Game developers and programmers
- Filmmakers and producers

- Musicians and composers
- Artisans and designers
- Architects and interior designers
- Scientists and researchers

Ultimately, all creative professions can benefit from using NFTs to protect and monetize their work.

NFT marketplaces and platforms

There are now a variety of NFT marketplaces and platforms where you can buy, sell, or even create NFTs. Here are some of the most popular ones:

1. OpenSea: OpenSea is one of the largest and most well-known NFT marketplaces. Here you can find a wide range of NFTs, including art, music, games and more.

2. Rarible: Rarible is an NFT platform where you can create, sell, and buy digital collectibles. The platform is built on Ethereum and offers a variety of tools for artists and buyers.

3. SuperRare: SuperRare is an NFT marketplace that specializes in digital artwork. The platform has a curated selection of artists and offers high-quality, limited edition digital artworks.

4. Nifty Gateway: Nifty Gateway is a platform that focuses on limited edition NFT artwork. The platform features artwork from some of the world's

most well-known artists and brands.

5. NBA Top Shot: NBA Top Shot is a platform that specializes in NFTs for sports fans. Here you can purchase collectibles from the NBA, including rare highlights and player photos.

6. Axie Infinity: Axie Infinity is a blockchain game based on the Ethereum blockchain. Here, you can breed, collect, and have digital pets (Axies) fight.

It's important to check out the fees, policies, and safety precautions before using an NFT platform or marketplace.

V. The future of NFTs

Forecasts and trends

NFTs have experienced tremendous growth in recent years, and the industry seems far from over. Here are some predictions and trends that could impact the future of NFTs:

NFTs are a relatively new technology that has gained traction in recent years. As with any new technology, there is a lot of speculation about how NFTs will evolve in the future. In this chapter, we take a look at some of the predictions and trends for NFTs.

1. growth of the NFT market

The NFT market has seen tremendous growth in recent years and experts agree that this is just the beginning. According to a study by NonFungible.com, the total value of the NFT market in 2020 was around 250 million US dollars. By the end of February 2021, that value had already increased to $340 million. Some forecasts predict that the NFT market will reach a value of 1.3 billion US dollars by 2025.

2. NFTs as a tool for content monetization

NFTs have the potential to create a new way to monetize digital content. Artists, musicians, authors, and other creators can use NFTs to sell digital works and profit directly from their work instead of relying on the sale of physical copies.

3. use of NFTs in the game industry

The use of NFTs in the gaming industry could be a big trend in the future. Game developers can use NFTs to create unique in-game items that players can collect and trade. These items could also be traded on other platforms, which would create a new income model for game developers.

4. NFTs as proof of identity

NFTs could also be used as proof of identity in the future. Because NFTs are unique and immutable, they can be used to verify digital identities, for example when logging on to online services or storing medical records.

5. further fields of application

Apart from the mentioned application areas, there are many other possibilities for NFTs. For example, they could be used in the real estate industry to manage the ownership of properties or in the fashion industry to verify the authenticity of clothing items.

Overall, the future prospects for NFTs are very promising. The technology has the potential to revolutionize various industries and create new opportunities for monetization and ownership. It will be interesting to observe how the use of NFTs evolves in the coming years.

Let's now take another look at some potential applications and developments that we should keep an eye on in the coming years:

- Virtual real estate: NFTs could soon serve as proof of ownership for virtual real estate. There are already virtual worlds like Decentraland and Somnium Space where users can purchase and develop virtual real estate. With NFTs as proof of ownership, these virtual plots of land could be bought, sold, and traded like real properties.
- Decentralized identity: NFTs could also be used to create a decentralized identity that is not tied to a central authority. Anyone could represent their identity through a chain of NFTs that serve as proof of certain skills, traits, or certifications.
- Integration into physical objects: NFTs could increasingly be integrated into physical objects in the future to guarantee their authenticity and make collectibles more valuable. For example, an NFT could serve as proof of ownership for a rare piece of artwork and be tied to the physical artwork.

- Gaming: NFTs have already gained importance in the gaming industry, but their potential applications are far from exhausted. In the future, NFTs could also serve as proof of progress in a game, as part of in-game purchases, or as virtual rewards for achievements.
- Energy efficiency: The high energy intensity of blockchain and NFTs has raised some criticism in the past. Therefore, some developers are already working on NFTs based on more energy-efficient blockchains to reduce the environmental impact.

These applications and developments are just a small fraction of the potential of NFTs. The technology is still young and it will be interesting to see how it evolves and what new application possibilities will arise in the future.

To become familiar with the various cryptocurrencies and blockchain platforms that can be used for the creation and trading of NFTs, one often requires a certain degree of technical knowledge, which can be a barrier for many investors.

Another technical issue that can arise with NFTs is scalability. As blockchain technology is still in its early stages, it is difficult to trade large quantities of NFTs at once without causing delays or overloads. Therefore, NFT platforms must develop scalable solutions to ensure that they can handle an increasing number of NFTs.

Another issue is the interoperability of NFTs across different blockchains and platforms. As there are currently no standardized protocols for NFTs, it can be difficult to transfer or trade NFTs between different platforms and blockchains. This can limit the liquidity of NFTs and make trading more challenging.

Regulatory Risks

As NFTs are still relatively new, there are also regulatory challenges and uncertainties, particularly regarding their legal classification and taxation. It is important to educate oneself about the applicable laws and regulations regarding the trading of NFTs in order to avoid legal issues and potential penalties.

In some countries, there are already efforts to regulate or restrict NFTs. Some governments have expressed concerns that NFTs could be used for illegal activities such as money laundering or trading stolen goods. Investors should be aware that regulatory changes can lead to changes in the demand and prices of NFTs.

Risks related to authenticity and verification

Another risk associated with NFTs is the authenticity and verification of digital assets. Since NFTs are based on blockchain technology, it is assumed that they are tamper-proof and have a unique identity. However, there are still possibilities for NFTs to be counterfeited or for their origin and authenticity not to be fully verified.

Investors must be aware that they may not be able to fully verify the origin or authenticity of an NFT, especially if it is an older or rare NFT. This can lead to issues with valuing NFTs and determining prices.

Volatility and price risks

Finally, like any other form of assets, NFTs are subject to price risks. The price of NFTs can fluctuate widely and depends on various factors such as demand, rarity of the NFT, and other market factors.

We will briefly address some points again in the following sections:

1. Scalability: The current infrastructure of blockchains can only handle limited amounts of transactions, which can lead to bottlenecks and high transaction costs. To make NFTs more accessible to a wider audience, scalability needs to be improved.

2. Interoperability: Since there are many different blockchains and NFT protocols, it can be difficult to move or trade NFTs between different platforms. There are efforts to establish standards to improve interoperability, but it remains a challenge.

3. Security: NFTs are digital and therefore can be vulnerable to theft and hacking. Storing NFTs therefore requires careful security planning, especially when using centralized exchanges.

4. Environmental impact: The mining of cryptocurrencies such as Bitcoin and Ethereum is energy-intensive and leads to high carbon emissions. This has an impact on the environment and can raise ethical concerns.

Despite these challenges, NFTs have the potential to change the way we perceive and utilize digital assets. If these challenges can be addressed, NFTs could become an important part of the future of the digital economy.

Market risks

As with any other asset, the value of NFTs is subject to fluctuations due to market factors such as supply and demand, public perception, market trends, and other economic and political events.

Technical Risks

As with any digital asset, the loss of passwords, damage to hardware devices, or the complexity of blockchain technology can result in NFTs being lost or inaccessible.

Fraud and Security Risks

Since NFTs are digital and traded online, there are also risks related to fraud and security. NFT investors need to be aware that there are scammers selling fake NFTs and that they need to be cautious to ensure they only buy from trusted sources..

Environmental Issues

Since NFTs are based on blockchain technology, as mentioned in a previous section, their production and trading will consume energy. The energy demand of blockchain technology is a well-known problem and has raised questions about the sustainability of cryptocurrencies and other digital assets.

Another risk factor for NFT investments is the volatility of the market. Since NFTs are still relatively new and their applications are still developing, the demand for certain NFTs can fluctuate greatly. An NFT that is fetching a high price today can lose value in a matter of weeks or months. Investors should therefore always have a diversified portfolio and not invest their entire capital in a single NFT position.

Another risk of NFT investments concerns regulation. Since the NFT market is still unregulated, governments and regulatory bodies may enact laws and regulations in the future that restrict or prohibit the trading of NFTs. Investors should stay informed about the regulatory landscape in their region and be prepared for potential changes.

In summary, NFT investments offer both opportunities and risks. Potential benefits include the ability to invest in unique digital assets and participate in the development of new applications. However, risks include the technical challenges in handling NFTs, market volatility, and uncertainty regarding future regulations. Investors should be aware of these risks and make an informed decision before investing in NFTs.

How to buy and sell NFTs

To buy or sell NFTs, one needs a cryptocurrency as most NFTs are based on the Ethereum blockchain and are typically paid for with Ether (ETH). Another important aspect is access to an NFT marketplace or platform where NFTs are traded.

In general, there are three ways to buy or sell NFTs:

NFT marketplaces: There are several NFT marketplaces, including OpenSea, Rarible, SuperRare, and Nifty Gateway, where one can buy and sell NFTs. These marketplaces typically offer a user-friendly interface and support various types of NFTs such as digital artworks, music pieces, and collectibles.

Auctions: Some NFTs are also sold through auction houses such as Christie's and Sotheby's. These auction houses have increasingly focused on NFTs in recent years and have achieved large sums for some of the most expensive NFTs.

Direct purchase and sale: It is also possible to buy or sell NFTs directly from an owner if one knows a potential buyer or seller.

Regardless of the method chosen, it is important to research the value of the NFT before making a purchase or sale. There are many factors that can affect the value of an NFT, including the artist's notoriety, the uniqueness of the NFT, and the demand on the market.

Due to the many advantages offered by NFTs, as well as the increasing acceptance by the general public and investors, it is expected that the NFT industry will continue to grow. Some experts predict that NFTs will play a role in almost every area of digital life in the future, from art, music, and sports to real estate and government agencies.

Some of the potential applications and developments of NFTs include:

• Using NFTs for the authentication of identities, possessions, and transactions

- Unlocking new business models and revenue streams for artists, musicians, and other creatives through the sale of NFTs as part of their creative process

- Using NFTs as a means of funding startups and other companies by selling NFTs to investors and using the proceeds for project development

- Using NFTs to manage supply chains and logistics by creating unique digital assets for products that can be tracked during the manufacturing process

- Using NFTs as a means of tokenizing assets such as real estate, artworks, and collectibles, providing investors access to a wider range of assets

- Introducing new types of NFTs that can represent a greater variety of digital assets, such as virtual properties or virtual pets.

Although the future of NFTs looks promising, there are still some challenges and uncertainties, particularly regarding the regulation of NFTs and the associated risks for investors. Nevertheless, it is clear that NFTs already have a significant impact on the digital world and will continue to grow and evolve in the future.

Another potential risk of NFT investments is the possibility of fraud or counterfeiting. Since NFTs are digital, it can be difficult to verify their authenticity, especially for NFTs representing digital artworks or other digital media. There are also reports of fake NFTs appearing on the market.

Another risk is that the market for NFTs can be very volatile and speculative, leading to high price fluctuations. Since the market is still relatively young, there are also fewer historical data to rely on for making predictions or analyzing trends.

Finally, there are also concerns about the environmental impact of NFTs, as the blockchain technology they rely on consumes a significant amount of energy. Some critics argue that the use of NFTs may be problematic due to these environmental impacts.

Overall, it is important for investors who want to acquire NFTs to carefully weigh these risks and conduct their own research to make informed decisions.

In conclusion, it can be said that while the use of NFTs has already encompassed a wide range of applications, there are also a number of developments that suggest that the use of NFTs will continue to grow in the future.

One of the developments that will play a role in the future is the integration of NFTs into virtual worlds and augmented reality applications. This could lead to even greater use of NFTs in the entertainment and gaming industries, and open up new opportunities for the creation and trading of virtual assets.

Another development we could see in the future is the use of NFTs as part of the authentication of physical objects. By using NFTs, it could be possible to prove the authenticity of physical objects such as artwork, collectibles, or even clothing. This could help reduce the market for counterfeit goods while also strengthening consumer trust in the trade of physical objects.

Another trend that will continue in the future is the increase of NFTs as instruments for financing projects and startups. NFTs can be used as a form of crowdfunding mechanism, where investors acquire digital assets and, in return, receive a share of the project's earnings.

Finally, we may also see NFTs used as a tool for creating social incentives in the future. For example, companies could use NFTs as rewards for employees who achieve certain performance goals or as part of loyalty programs to reward customers.

Overall, there are many ways in which NFTs can be used in the future, and it is likely that their use will continue to increase in the coming years. The technology and market are still in development, and it remains to be seen how things will evolve in the future.

1. Interoperability: One of the biggest challenges for NFTs is that they often only work on a

specific platform or blockchain. Interoperability, however, will become increasingly important as NFTs may be used in different applications and ecosystems.

2. Mass appeal: Currently, NFTs are mainly known among collectors and cryptocurrency enthusiasts. However, a broader acceptance and spread of NFTs could help them become a mainstream phenomenon in the future.

3. Improved interoperability: Some experts predict that in the future, various NFTs will be interoperable, meaning they can be easily transferred between different blockchains. This would increase the flexibility of NFTs and allow users to use multiple NFTs on different platforms.

4. Integration into games: NFTs could also play an important role in the gaming industry, especially in relation to in-game assets and properties. Game developers could use NFTs to promote and reward ownership and control of in-game assets.

NFTs are currently mainly prevalent in the art and culture industry, but there are already numerous applications in other industries such as music, video games, and sports. In the future, further areas of application could be explored, such as education or virtual real estate.

5.

6. Art and culture: NFTs have already had a significant impact on the art and culture industry, and it is likely that this trend will continue in the future. Artists and creatives can use NFTs to monetize their work and create new sources of income. In the future, NFTs could become the standard for the sale and management of artworks, and museums could include digital artworks in their collections.

7.

8. More applications in the music industry: NFTs offer artists the opportunity to have more control over their music and earnings. In the future, NFTs could be used to manage music

rights and provide fans with access to exclusive content.

9.

10.Growing importance in the sports world: NFTs can also play an important role in the sports industry. They could be used to confirm the authenticity of sports memorabilia and provide fans with access to exclusive content and experiences.

11.

12.Tokenization of physical assets: NFTs can also help tokenize physical assets such as artworks, real estate, and other collectibles, enabling faster and more efficient transfers.

13.NFTs in der DeFi: Ein weiterer Trend ist die Integration von NFTs in dezentralisierten Finanzanwendungen (DeFi). NFTs could, for example, be used as collateral for loans or as part of decentralized marketplaces and exchanges.

14.14. Advances in blockchain technology: The development of NFTs is closely related to blockchain technology. Advances in blockchain technology can help make NFTs faster, more secure, and more efficient.

15.

16.Development of NFT ecosystems: In the future, complex NFT ecosystems could be developed that connect different NFTs and create new application possibilities. These ecosystems could consist of different platforms, marketplaces, smart contracts, and other technologies that together provide a seamless and scalable infrastructure for NFTs.

17.Environmental awareness: The issue of sustainability will also play a role in the future. Some critics have highlighted the high energy costs and associated environmental footprint of NFTs. One possible solution is to create NFTs on more environmentally friendly blockchains or technologies.

18.Regulation: Given the rapid growth of NFTs, there may soon be greater regulation, particularly in relation to taxes, intellectual property, and data protection.

19. The future of NFTs is promising, but there are also challenges that need to be addressed. One of the biggest challenges is the lack of regulation in this area. Since NFTs are a new concept, there are no clear regulations and standards yet. There is a risk that fraudsters will exploit the uncertainty and deceive investors.
20. Another challenge is that NFTs are a relatively new concept, and it is not yet clear how the market will develop. The NFT market is very volatile and it is difficult to predict which NFTs will gain or lose value in the future.
21. Despite these challenges, many experts see a promising future for NFTs. Some suggest that NFTs could soon become an integral part of our lives.

Potential Applications and Developments

NFTs have already shown a variety of applications in different areas, but there is still a lot of potential for future developments and applications. Here are some possible developments and applications of NFTs:

1. Virtual worlds: NFTs could be used in virtual worlds like Second Life or Decentraland to facilitate the trade of digital items and properties.

2. Identity management: NFTs could also be used for secure management of identity data. An example of this is Microsoft's digital identity project, which uses NFTs to secure identity credentials.

3. Supply chain management: NFTs could be used in the supply chain to simplify and improve the tracking of goods and products.

4. Authenticity certificates: NFTs can also be used as authenticity certificates for physical assets such as artworks, collectibles, and luxury goods.

5. Asset tokenization: NFTs could also be used for the tokenization of assets such as stocks, real estate, and other asset classes to facilitate trading and transfer.

6. Decentralized identity: NFTs could also be used to create a decentralized identity, where individuals maintain control over their identity data and store it on a decentralized blockchain.

7. Collaborative creation: NFTs could also be used in the future for the collaborative creation of digital content such as music, art, and video games by documenting and rewarding each creator's contribution to the creation of a digital asset.

In fact, NFTs have already gained remarkable attention and acceptance in a short period of time, and have shown that they could be an important component of the future of the digital economy. It will be exciting to see how the technology and applications of NFTs will continue to evolve in the coming years..

VII. Conclusion: Are NFTs the future?

It's hard to say whether NFTs are the future or not, as the technology is still relatively new and there is still a lot of room for development and innovation. However, there are already numerous use cases for NFTs in various industries, from art and music to sports and gaming.

Some experts believe that NFTs are a transformative technology that represent a transformation in the way we own, share, and trade digital content. Others, however, are skeptical and see NFTs as a passing fad that will only be relevant for a limited time.

It is important to note that NFTs are not without challenges and risks. Investors should be aware that the market for NFTs is volatile and unpredictable, and there may be difficulties in finding buyers for certain NFTs. In addition, there are technical challenges and questions regarding the environmental impact of NFTs.

Despite these challenges, there are also numerous opportunities and potentials for NFTs. Investors should familiarize themselves with the technology and carefully consider whether they want to invest in the NFT market.

Overall, NFTs are an exciting new technology that has the potential to change the way we own and trade digital content. Whether they are the future or not remains to be seen, but it is clear that they have already had a significant impact on the world of digital assets.

VIII. Conclusion

Summary of key insights

In this book, we have explored non-fungible tokens (NFTs) and their definition, history, applications, and future potential. We have found that NFTs represent unique digital assets secured through blockchain technology. By using smart contracts, NFTs can be uniquely programmed to fulfill specific conditions and properties.

We have examined the various applications of NFTs, including art and culture, music, the video game industry, sports, and social media. We have also discussed the opportunities and risks of NFT investments, including the potential for high returns but also the risks of market volatility and fraud.

Finally, we have explored the potential of NFTs for future developments and applications, including the use of NFTs in virtual worlds, identity management, supply chain management, authenticity certificates, tokenization of assets, decentralized identity, and collaborative creation.

However, there are also challenges and risks associated with NFT investments. Prices can be volatile, and there are concerns about the sustainability and environmental impact of the blockchain technology that supports NFTs.

Overall, we have found that NFTs represent an exciting new concept in the world of digital assets and have enormous potential for creating new markets and applications.

Some of the key insights we gained from this study include:

• NFTs are digital assets that are based on blockchain technology and are unique and immutable.

• NFTs have a long history that dates back to the early days of blockchain technology, but have only recently gained significance due to the popularity of cryptocurrencies and DeFi applications.

- Compared to other digital assets, NFTs offer unique features such as immutability and uniqueness that make them attractive to artists and collectors.
- Investors should be aware that NFTs can be highly volatile and there is no guarantee that they will maintain or increase in value.
- Technical challenges such as high gas fees and scalability can restrict the use of NFTs and make buying and selling NFTs difficult.
- There are various ways to buy and sell NFTs, including NFT marketplaces and platforms such as OpenSea, Nifty Gateway, and SuperRare.
- NFTs have the potential to be used in various industries, such as the music, art, and gaming industries.

It is important for investors and users to conduct thorough research and be aware that NFTs are not a guaranteed investment. The technology is still in development and there is much to learn and improve.

However, NFTs have already had a significant impact on the art world and other industries, and it is clear that they will play an important role in the future. The technology enables a new type of ownership and tradability of digital content and has the potential to revolutionize creative industries.

Overall, NFTs represent an exciting and promising new chapter in the world of digital assets. It will be exciting to see how this market develops in the coming years and what impact it will have on various industries.

Personal Assessment and Recommendations

My personal assessment is that NFTs are a promising and exciting concept that will play an important role in the future. Particularly in areas such as art, music, and sports, NFTs can bring a revolutionary change by allowing artists and athletes to sell their digital works and collectibles directly to their fans.

As an investment opportunity, while NFTs offer the chance for high returns, there are also risks to consider, such as market volatility and fraud. Therefore, it's important for potential investors to thoroughly research NFTs and the associated risks before investing.

My recommendation for those interested in NFTs is to continue to educate themselves and possibly even buy NFTs themselves to get a better understanding of how they work and what applications exist. Additionally, it's advisable to watch out for reputable

NFT marketplaces and platforms and not fall for fraudulent offers.

Overall, I see NFTs as an exciting new development in the world of digital assets and look forward to seeing how this technology evolves and brings forth new applications.

VIIII. Anhang

Glossar

Here is a glossary with some important terms related to NFTs:

1. Blockchain: A distributed digital database that records transactions and enables secure digital assets.
2. Ethereum: A decentralized blockchain platform where smart contracts can be executed and NFTs can be created.
3. IPFS: The InterPlanetary File System is a decentralized peer-to-peer file system used to store NFT metadata.
4. Gas: A unit of fee required on the Ethereum blockchain for the execution of smart contracts.
5. Cryptocurrency: A digital currency that uses cryptographic technology to secure and manage transactions.
6. Metamask: A browser extension used as a wallet for Ethereum and NFTs.

7. Mining: The process of processing transactions on a blockchain, where new units of a cryptocurrency are created.
8. NFT: Non-Fungible Token, a unique digital token that is not interchangeable and serves as proof of ownership for digital content.
9. NFT marketplaces: Online platforms where NFTs can be bought and sold.
10. Non-fungible: Not interchangeable or replaceable.
11. OpenSea: An NFT marketplace where NFTs can be bought and sold.
12. NFT: Non-Fungible Token, a unique digital token that is non-exchangeable and serves as proof of ownership for digital content.
13. NFT marketplaces: Online platforms where NFTs can be bought and sold.
14. Non-fungible: Non-exchangeable or irreplaceable.
15. OpenSea: An NFT marketplace where NFTs can be bought and sold.
16. Proof-of-Work: A consensus mechanism used in some blockchains where participants must

solve complex mathematical problems to validate transactions and create new units of a cryptocurrency.

17. Proof-of-Stake: An alternative consensus mechanism where participants must hold units of a cryptocurrency to validate transactions and create new units.

18. Rarible: Another NFT marketplace where artists and collectors can sell digital assets.

19. Smart Contract: A self-executing code that runs on a blockchain platform and can trigger transactions automatically.

20. Token: A digital object that exists on a blockchain platform.

21. Tokenization: The process of converting physical or digital assets into tokens. A digital representation of assets stored on a blockchain.

22. Wallet: A digital wallet used to store cryptocurrencies and NFTs.

This glossary is intended to serve as a reference and is not exhaustive. There are many other terms and concepts related to NFTs that you may discover as you learn more about this fascinating technology.

Known NFT offerings

Everydays: The First 5000 Days

Everydays: The First 5000 Days is a digital artwork created by Mike Winkelmann, professionally known as Beeple. The work is a collage of 5000 digital images that Winkelmann created for his Everydays series. The associated non-fungible token (NFT) was sold at Christie's in 2021 for $69.3 million, making it the most expensive non-fungible token of all time.

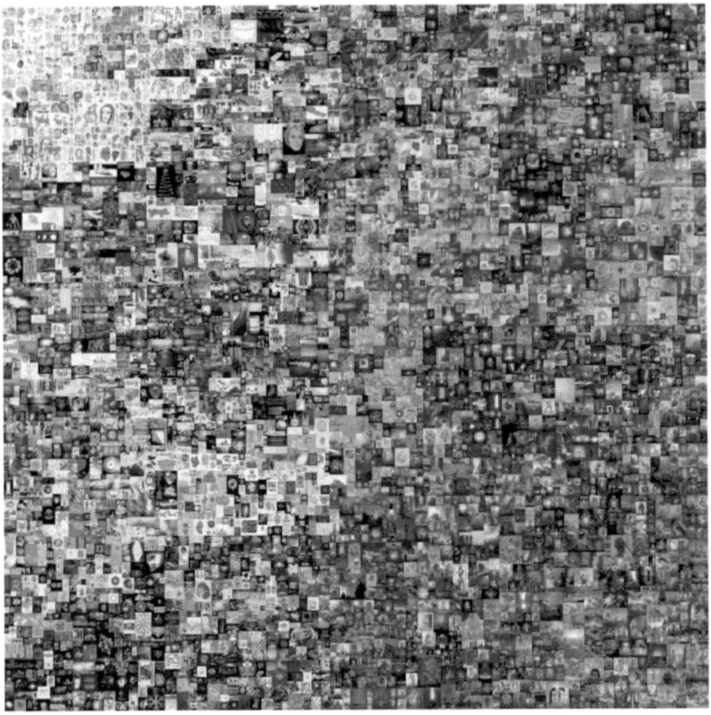

Quelle: https://www.arshake.com/en/frame-everydays-the-first-5000-days/

Everydays was purchased by Singapore-based programmer Vignesh Sundaresan, a cryptocurrency investor and the founder of the Metapurse NFT project, who is also known online under his pseudonym MetaKovan. Sundaresan paid for the artwork with 42,329 Ether. Both the buyer Sundaresan and the seller Winkelmann had an interest in driving up the price of the work to draw attention to a speculative asset that was associated with twenty other Beeple works, which they called "B20 tokens." The price of these tokens, in which Sundaresan held a majority stake, reached its peak during the media coverage of the Everydays auction and subsequently collapsed, leading some observers to label the auction as a publicity stunt and a scam.

One of the 5000 images that make up the artwork.

Quelle: By Mike Winkelmann - behance.net (licence), CC BY 4.0, https://commons.wikimedia.org/w/index.php?curid=86000833

Sundaresan has the rights to exhibit the artwork, but not the copyright. He has exhibited the artworks in a digital museum in the "metaverse" that the public can view through a web browser.

Bibliography:

Here is a list of books, articles, and websites that have been used as references for this book on NFTs:

Books:

- Aitkenhead, D. (2021). NFT: The Future of Digital Art. Thames & Hudson.
- Chiu, J., & Koeppl, T. (2021). NFTs and Beyond: A Brief Survey of Blockchain-Based Digital Art Marketplaces. Review of Economic Dynamics, 39, 264-286.
- Buterin, V. (2014). A next-generation smart contract and decentralized application platform. Ethereum White Paper, 1-32.
- Dieterich, W. (2021). Non-Fungible Tokens (NFTs) – Ein Überblick. Steuerliche Aspekte. Verlag Otto Schmidt.
- Heston, J. (2021). NFTs: A Simple Guide for Creators and Collectors. Packt Publishing Ltd.

- Hockenos, P. (2021). NFT Art: Investieren Sie in die Zukunft des Kunstmarktes. Independently published.
- Howcroft, E. (2021). NFTs Explained: What They Are, and Why They're Selling for Millions of Dollars. The Guardian.
- Jentzsch, C. (2018). Introducing Ethereum and Solidity: Foundations of Cryptocurrency and Blockchain Programming for Beginners. Apress.
- Peck, M. (2018). What's an NFT? And Why Are People Paying Millions for Them? Wired.
- Tapscott, D., & Tapscott, A. (2016). Blockchain Revolution: How the Technology Behind Bitcoin is Changing Money, Business, and the World. Penguin Random House.

Artikel:

- Alpeyev, P., & Leising, M. (2021, March 11). The NFT Craze Is Here. Is It Over? Bloomberg.
- Delaney, K. (2021, March 8). What Are NFTs? The New Bitcoin, Explained. Wired.
- Lee, D. (2021, February 19). NFTs Explained: What They Are, and Why They're Booming. BBC.
- Ray, T. (2021, March 17). NFTs: Everything You Need to Know about Non-Fungible Tokens. CNET.

Websites:

- OpenSea: https://opensea.io/
- Rarible: https://rarible.com/
- CryptoKitties: https://www.cryptokitties.co/
- Ethereum: https://ethereum.org/
- IPFS: https://ipfs.io/
- SuperRare: https://superrare.co/
- Nifty Gateway: https://niftygateway.com/

This list is not exhaustive, but it provides a good starting point for further reading and research.

Links and Resources

Here are some additional links and resources on the topic of NFTs:

- Non-Fungible.com: https://www.nonfungible.com/ - Ein Portal providing the latest NFT data and statistics.
- NFTs on Reddit: https://www.reddit.com/r/NFT/ - An active Reddit community focused on NFTs.
- The Nifty Gateway: https://niftygateway.com/ - A marketplace for NFTs supported by the Winklevoss twins.
- SuperRare: https://superrare.co/ - A marketplace for digital art NFTs.
- Foundation: https://foundation.app/ - Another marketplace for NFTs with a focus on digital art.
- NFT Showroom: https://nftshowroom.com/ - A marketplace specializing in NFTs related to crypto art..

- CryptoPunks: https://www.larvalabs.com/cryptopunks - One of the first and most well-known collections of NFTs..
- NBA Top Shot: https://www.nbatopshot.com/ - An NFT marketplace that focuses on digital NBA collectible cards.
- Mirror: https://mirror.xyz/ - A platform for NFTs that allows users to create tokens representing various types of content..
- "The Future of NFTs" (Forbes-Artikel): https://www.forbes.com/sites/roberthart/2021/02/26/the-future-of-nfts/ - An article discussing the potential applications of NFTs in various industries.

These links and resources provide a variety of information and insights into the world of NFTs..

Impressum:

Holger Kiefer
Kopernikusstr. 14
D-90766 Fürth
beratungholgerkiefer@gmx.de

https://kiefer-coaching.de
https://heil-weg.de
https://kinder-angst.de

Noizcn:

Notice

Notice